Transfer at eleven

allocation in comprehensive and selective systems 1971/72

Christopher J. Hill
Research officer, NFER

NFER

*Published by the National Foundation for Educational Research
in England and Wales*

Registered Office: The Mere, Upton Park, Slough, Bucks, SL1 2DQ

*Book Publishing Division: 2 Jennings Buildings, Thames Avenue,
Windsor, Berks, SL4 1QS*

First Published 1972

© *National Foundation for Educational Research,* 1972

0036835
SBN 0901225 99 1

Cover design by
Peter Gauld, FSIA

Printed in Great Britain by
Direct Design (Bournemouth) Ltd., 12 Roumelia Lane, Boscombe,
Bournemouth, Hampshire

Contents

List of Tables

List of Diagrams

CHAPTER ONE
Introduction

1. *The objectives of the study*
   This is the report of a study of procedures used by local education authorities to allocate pupils to secondary schools. Surveys on this topic have now been made by the National Foundation for Educational Research at roughly four-year intervals since 1952.[1] In the past they have concentrated upon the methods used to select pupils for grammar schools: in this survey the focus has shifted and more questions have been asked about issues related to the growth of comprehensive education. The study therefore divides into two main sections; the first, discussed in Chapter Two, covers the same area as the previous study; the second, in Chapter Three, investigates comprehensive systems and mixed systems where grammar and comprehensive schools co-exist. As in previous surveys, the findings are based upon replies to a questionnaire sent out to all Chief Education Officers and other documentary evidence supplied by the authorities concerning their present practices.

   The first part of the questionnaire replicated exactly many of the questions from the 1968 survey. It concerns the various types of information collected for selective allocation, the ways in which this information is combined and what procedures are used to handle age and sex differences.

   Where a selective system occurs, the procedure is normally one of allocating each pupil a place at either a grammar or a secondary modern school. No distinction is made for other types of school, such as technical schools, these being treated where applicable together with grammar schools as 'selective schools'.

   As this is one of a series of studies, an attempt has been made to show the trends over a period of·20 years. This objective is, however, limited by variations in the form of the questions asked by successive surveys. To improve comparability, many questions in this survey were identical to those used in 1968. For some information, where the alternatives are

[1] NFER (1964). *Local Authority Practices in the Allocation of Pupils to Secondary Education.* Slough: NFER.
NFER (1968). *Trends in Allocation Procedures.* Slough: NFER.

clear-cut and unambiguous, changes in the wording of questions may not seriously have affected the comparability of results: elsewhere, as is indicated in the text, practices are more difficult to categorize and consequently the results must be interpreted more cautiously.

An initial question in the survey sought to divide authorities into three main groups:

(1)   Those with a selective procedure throughout their area.
(2)   Those with a selective procedure in only part of their area.
(3)   Those with no selective procedure.

This classification in the main coincides with a classification of authorities by the type of secondary school system they administer. The three categories above can be restated as:

(1)   Authorities with grammar and secondary modern schools and in which comprehensive schools are few or non-existent.
(2)   Authorities that are divided into areas, some with comprehensive schools predominating and some with predominantly grammar and secondary modern schools.
(3)   Authorities with essentially total comprehensive systems.

In Chapter Three details are given of the prevalence of various types of comprehensive system and the rate of reorganization. As will be shown, a large number of authorities now have grammar, secondary modern and comprehensive schools. This raises a number of issues as to how pupils are allocated between different systems and whether the systems occur in the same or different areas. It also raises the question as to which pupils undergo an allocation procedure and whether pupils may opt in or out of a comprehensive system. Some interesting points emerge on these problems.

2. *The questionnaire*

As most authorities' practices are sufficiently standard to be simply classified, a precoded questionnaire was used. Spaces were also provided to allow comments to be written in. These were used by authorities to indicate their practices where they did not fall into specified categories or where there was some diversity of procedure in their area. This also gave an opportunity to determine possible new trends.

A common theme of these comments was that the questionnaire forced them into categories that suggested a formality which belied the real flexibility of their system. The main points raised included:

(1)   The use of parental choice as against formalized tests to determine allocation.
(2)   The extent to which local variations occurred within their area.
(3)   The detail with which borderline candidates are investigated.

(4)   The extent to which head teachers are drawn into close co-operation in the whole process.

Certain authorities indicated that the nature of what information was collected on candidates was the responsibility of the panel of local head teachers. The value of such flexibility and diversity must, however, be carefully assessed. The formal system may be impartially just or unjust, whereas a flexible system, while sensitive to particular needs, may also be sensitive to particular local pressure.

The number of authorities that found difficulties in fitting to the pre-coded pattern was, however, small and the duplication of questions given in the previous survey allowed comparisons over time.

As indicated above, this report includes some findings from past studies. More detail can be found by direct reference to these, particularly the 1964 study. The information from past surveys used in this report has been selected for the purpose of bringing out more clearly certain trends. These trends are very well defined, though in interpreting them account must be taken of the effects of local authority reorganizations, such as the creation of the 20 Outer London Boroughs between the 1964 and 1968 surveys.

3. *Classification of the authorities*

The questionnaire was sent to all LEAs except the Isle of Man. The authorities were classified into three groups, County Councils, County Boroughs and Welsh authorities. Questionnaires were not returned by only two authorities, both County Boroughs. This left a total of 161, of which 97 were County Boroughs, 47 County Councils and 17 Welsh authorities.

The Welsh authorities, which are grouped together throughout, consist of 13 County Councils and four County Boroughs.

CHAPTER TWO

Systems of Selection

How do local authorities determine which pupils are to be allocated grammar school places? The decision as to which method is used is essentially in the hands of each authority and there is considerable diversity of practice. In most cases the procedure adheres to certain standard patterns, though a few LEAs have developed their own methods. In this chapter a description will be given of the methods used, with details of both the present extent of these practices and the major changes in recent years.

Normally, the procedure goes through the following stages:

(1)   Information is collected on some or all the pupils in the appropriate age group.

(2)   This information is then used to allocate the substantial majority of pupils to either grammar or secondary modern schools.

(3)   For a small number of pupils, a further investigation is made before final allocation. These pupils commonly described as belonging to the 'borderzone group' are those close to the selection boundary or those for whom some doubt has been raised as to their correct placement.

This third stage may entail further collection of information on certain pupils, though elsewhere all that is required for the borderzone procedure is collected at the outset.

The following list gives the main sources used by local authorities:

(1)   Formal tests of English, mathematics and verbal reasoning.
(2)   Essays.
(3)   Teachers' assessments.
(4)   Record cards.
(5)   Interviews of pupils, teachers or parents.

Each of these was investigated and is discussed below.

Though a number of types of data may have been collected, these are then used to determine the single decision of allocation. The authorities must therefore adopt some technique of combining this information. As will be seen below, verbal reasoning tests and teachers' assessments are the principal criteria used in the main allocation procedure. Further details are therefore given as to how these are used in combination.

The other aspects of allocation which are investigated in further detail are the methods used to take account of age and sex differences.

1. *Eligibility*

With the development of comprehensive schools, many pupils now continue to secondary education without experiencing a selective allocation procedure. Though there are issues involved in allocation to alternative comprehensives, this is not the concern of this chapter. Normally, therefore, the usages 'allocation' and 'procedure' will refer to selective systems, and those authorities or areas described as having 'no procedure' are ones that have adopted comprehensive systems.

As was, however, revealed by the 1964 survey, a number of authorities applied an allocation procedure in parts of their areas only. The 1968 questionnaire therefore included a question asking authorities to indicate the extensiveness of their procedures. The 1972 questionnaire repeated this. A classification of replies is given in Table 1.

Table 1: *Authorities using allocation procedures*

EXTENT OF ALLOCATION PROCEDURE	ENGLISH* CCs		ENGLISH* CBs		WALES		TOTAL	
	No.	%	No.	%	No.	%	No.	%
1. No procedure	6	13	33	34	11	65	50	31
2. Procedure in part of area only	36	77	15	15	5	29	56	35
3. Procedure in whole area	5	10	49	50	1	6	55	34
Total	47	100	97	100	17	100	161	100

* In subsequent tables these are referred to simply as 'CCs' and 'CBs'.

The results indicate a continuation of the trend shown in 1968 (see Diagram 1). In 1964 only two authorities had no procedure, by 1968 the number was 26, in 1972 it is 50. Though this is a substantial increase, it still represents less than a third of all authorities. Certain aspects of this trend and information as to possible future trends are given in more detail in a later section.

10

The differences between the three types of authorities are similar to those shown in 1968. Wales has proceeded further towards abolishing allocation procedure. The characteristic feature of County Councils noted in the last report was the extent to which they have an allocation procedure in only part of their authority. This characteristic has now increased and is true of 77 per cent compared with 56 per cent in 1968. There is also an increase in the number of Boroughs in this category. The contrast between the two types of authorities has, however, if anything, increased.

Diagram 1: *Changes in the proportion of authorities using allocation procedures*

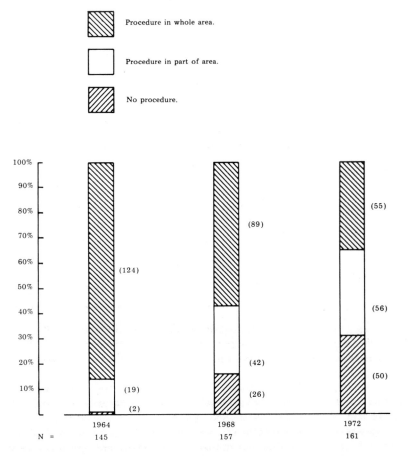

NB: Numbers of authorities in each category are given in brackets

The finding can undoubtedly be put down to 'on the one hand, the compactness of County Borough areas and, on the other hand, the heterogeneity of County areas', as stated in a previous report.

2. *Use of tests*
Three types of tests are used. These are in:
(1)   Verbal reasoning (intelligence tests).
(2)   English.
(3)   Mathematics or arithmetic.

The use of attainment tests in both English and in mathematics continues to decline. There has been a marked drop in the number and proportion of authorities using these tests. By contrast, there has been little change in the use of verbal reasoning (intelligence) tests apart from that due to the complete abolition of an allocation procedure. Of those 111 authorities practising an allocation procedure, 105 use tests and all those use a test of verbal reasoning. Table 2 indicates the distribution of authorities using tests. (The tables in this section refer only to authorities with an allocation procedure.)

Table 2: *Authorities using any tests*

WHETHER TEST GIVEN	CCs		CBs		WALES		TOTAL	
	No.	*%*	*No.*	*%*	*No.*	*%*	*No.*	*%*
Yes	38	93	61	95	6	100	105	95
No	3	7	3	5	0	0	6	5
Total with procedure	41	100	64	100	6	100	111	100

The decline in the use of an English test has been from 120 in 1964, to 67 in 1968 and 34 in 1972. Similarly, in mathematics the decline is from 118 in 1964, to 62 in 1968 and 27 in 1972. These changes are illustrated by Diagram 2.

Admission to Grammar Schools (Yates and Pidgeon, 1957) recommended the use of tests of verbal reasoning combined with teachers' assessments. This recommendation was based upon research findings that such a procedure predicted performance at secondary schools as well as any other. Later in this report it will be shown that teacher assessments are also widely used. It seems clear that this recommendation is still largely followed.

Diagram 2: *Of those authorities with an allocation procedure, changes in the proportions using tests.*

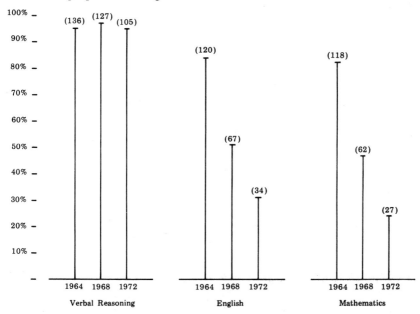

N.B. 1) Numbers of authorities in each category are given in brackets.
2) Total numbers of authorities with allocation procedures are:
1964 — 143; 1968 — 131; 1972 — 111.

Table 3: *Authorities using verbal or verbal reasoning tests*

SOURCE OF TEST	CCs No.	CBs No.	WALES No.	TOTAL No.	%
1. NFER or Moray House only	31	53	2	86	78
2. NFER or Moray House with other tests	8	7	3	18	16
3. Other test only	0	0	1	1	1
4. No verbal test	2	4	0	6	5
Total with procedure	41	64	6	111	100

It is also evident that there has been little change in the reliance upon professional test makers. Standardized tests are produced by the NFER and Moray House for allocation at 11+ and only a small proportion of authorities use other tests, either alone or with standardized ones. Tables 3, 4 and 5 indicate the present position.

Table 4: *Authorities using English tests*

SOURCE OF TEST	CCs	CBs	WALES	TOTAL	
	No.	No.	No.	No.	%
1. NFER or Moray House only	5	16	1	22	20
2. NFER or Moray House with other tests	2	3	3	8	7
3. Other test only	1	2	1	4	4
4. No English test	33	43	1	77	70
Total with procedure	41	64	6	111	100

Table 5: *Authorities using mathematics test*

SOURCE OF TEST	CCs	CBs	WALES	TOTAL	
	No.	No.	No.	No.	%
1. NFER or Moray House only	5	12	1	18	16
2. NFER or Moray House with other tests	1	2	1	4	4
3. Other test only	1	3	1	5	4
2. No maths test	34	47	3	84	76
Total with procedure	41	64	6	111	100

3. *Use of essays*

The use of essays by authorities continues to decline. During the period surveys have been carried out, the number of authorities using essays has steadily dropped from a high point of 75 per cent in 1956 to only 24 per cent in 1972 (see Diagram 3). The current position is indicated in Table 6.

The use of these essays is much as in 1968. Only 13 authorities mark all the essays. The procedure elsewhere is to use essays only as supplementary evidence such as in a borderzone procedure.

Diagram 3: *The percentage of authorities with an allocation procedure that used essays*

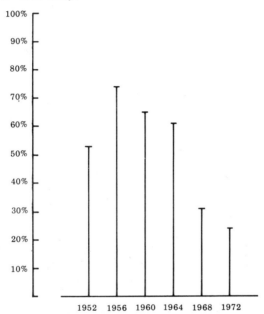

4. *Teachers' assessments*

Research has shown scaled primary teachers' assessments to be the best single predictor of secondary school success. That this is so does not necessarily mean that these are objective but rather that factors which affect teachers' assessments are akin to those that affect subsequent achievement. There is indeed a growing body of research evidence upon the relationship between teacher expectations and pupil performance. Also teachers' assessments are the responsibility of the head teacher. No inquiry was made as to how far other teachers are committed and as to whether an authority gives any instructions regarding this.

However, the use of teacher assessment remains a major feature of allocation procedures and hence of the surveys, especially since 1960,

Table 6: *Authorities using essays and the practices they employ*

	CCs	CBs	WALES	TOTAL
	No.	No.	No.	No.
Using essays	12	13	2	27
For all candidates	6	11	2	19
For some candidates only	6	2	0	8
All are marked	5	7	1	13
Some are marked	2	5	0	7
None are marked	5	1	1	7
Total with procedure	41	64	6	111

when the first survey after the publication of the NFER report *Admission to Grammar Schools* was conducted. An analysis of replies received in response to questions about the use of teachers' assessments in the 1972 questionnaire is presented in this section, beginning with Table 7, which shows the number of authorities using teachers' assessments in various ways. The results were similar to those in the previous study.

Only one authority reported that it did not obtain teachers' assessments. The figures indicate a widespread use of teachers' assessments among authorities who still operate an allocation procedure.

Such changes as have occurred are small. With fewer authorities operating a procedure the numbers in most categories are smaller. The slight changes in percentages may be due not so much to authorities actually changing their practices as to differences in the proportions in each category in 1968 that have now abolished allocation. Eighty-five authorities obtain and use assessments for all pupils, 22 use them for only some pupils. Those using teachers' assessments for only some pupils normally indicate their use either for borderzone pupils or borderzone pupils and above.

Teachers' assessments can be obtained in very many different ways. The questionnaire therefore attempted to distinguish between authorities who use overall rank orders of suitability for grammar school education and authorities who use some other procedure. Among the latter are included authorities who use orders of merit or gradings for separate subjects. Table 8 shows a classification of replies.

Table 7: *Authorities using primary teachers' assessments*

	CCs	CBs	WALES	TOTAL	
	No.	*No.*	*No.*	*No.*	*%*
1. Obtained and used for all pupils	30	50	5	85	79
2. Obtained for all, used only for some	5	4	1	10	9
3. Obtained and used only for some	6	6	0	12	11
4. Not obtained	0	1	0	1	1
Total with procedure	41	61	6	108	100

N.B. (1) Three County Boroughs gave no reply to questions analysed in Table 7.

(2) Tables 8 and 9 give analysis of questions which would only be answered by authorities classified as 1, 2 or 3 in Table 7.

Overall rank orders of suitability can be readily scaled and quantified so that the resulting 'score' can be used like a test score, and if required, added to other test scores. A method for doing this (referred to as 'Method A')[1] was outlined on pages 85-93 of *Admission to Grammar Schools*. An alternative way of using teachers' assessment (referred to as 'Method B')[2] does not involve scaling and quantifying them. This method was described on pages 121-6 of *Admission to Grammar Schools*. There are also other ways in which teachers' assessments can be used in an unscaled and unquantified form. Table 9 shows the numbers and percentages of authorities who were using teachers' assessments in various ways in 1972. Only authorities who used overall rank orders of suitability were

[1] METHOD A. Pupils are ranked by the head teacher and obtain a score on the verbal reasoning test. The pupil's scaled assessment is then determined by attributing to him the test score which has the same rank order position as he has been given by the head teacher.

[2] METHOD B. Pupils are classified as 'grammar', 'doubtful', 'modern' by the head teacher and also by the test scores. These combined give nine categories. These categories are then used to determine allocation, with possible further investigation for borderzone candidates.

asked to detail the use they made of teachers' assessments, but a comparison of the total numbers in Table 9 with the numbers in Table 8 indicates that a few more authorities than expected offered details.

Table 8: *Authorities employing different procedures in obtaining teachers' assessments*

PROCEDURE	CCs	CBs	WALES	TOTAL	
	No.	*No.*	*No.*	*No.*	*%*
1. Rank orders of suitability to grammar schools	29	48	5	82	84
2. Some other procedure	7	4	0	11	11
3. Rank orders and other procedure	2	3	0	5	5
Total No. of LEAs concerned	38	55	5	98	100

NB. (1) Tables 8 and 9 give analysis of questions which would only be answered by authorities classified as 1, 2 or 3 in Table 7.

     (2) Ten authorities gave no reply to the question analysed in Table 8.

Age Allowances

When asking teachers to make assessments, authorities can instruct them either to take age into account to offset the tendency to give higher ratings to the older children, or to ignore the age factor, and then apply a correction for age when scaling and quantifying the assessments. There is, of course, a third choice — authorities can refrain from giving any instructions to their teachers at all. The numbers of authorities taking these different lines of action are given in Table 10.

As Table 10 and Diagram 4 show, more than half the authorities give no instructions about age allowance, and there have been only slight changes in the proportions.

The report *Admission to Grammar Schools* suggested on pages 92-93 three methods which could be used when orders of suitability were employed and scaling was carried out by Method A (see Table 9 and

Table 9: *Authorities scaling and quantifying rank orders of suitability by different methods*

METHOD	CCs No.	CBs No.	WALES No.	TOTAL No.	%
1. Scaled and quantified according to Method A	15	27	2	44	48
2. Scaled and quantified by some other method	3	3	1	7	8
3. Used according to Method B	5	6	0	11	12
4. Used unscaled, unquantified in some other way	11	16	2	29	32
Total No. of LEAs concerned	34	52	5	91	100

NB. (1)   Tables 8 and 9 give analysis of questions which would only be answered by authorities classified as 1, 2 or 3 in Table 7.
     (2)   Seventeen authorities gave no reply to the question analysed in Table 9.

Table 10: *Teachers' assessments: authorities giving different instructions with regard to pupils' ages*

	CCs No.	CBs No.	WALES No.	TOTAL No.	%
1. Instructed to make allowances for age differences	5	14	1	20	20
2. Instructed not to make allowances for age differences	10	15	0	25	24
3. Not given any instruction with regard to age	25	29	4	58	56
Total with procedure	40	58	5	103	100

Eight authorities gave no reply to the question analysed in Table 10.

Diagram 4: *Changes in the proportions making age allowances*

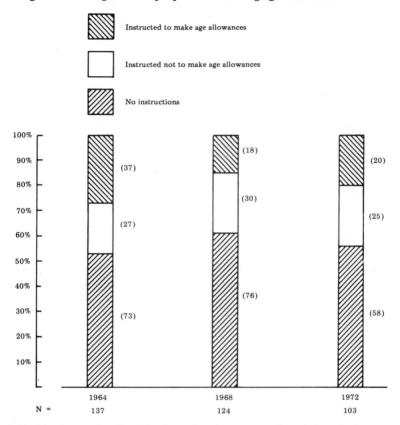

NB: Numbers of authorities in each category are given in brackets.

accompanying text). The methods suggested were as follows:

(a)   calculating the average quantified assessment at each month of age, and so determining the average increase per month of age;
(b)   using the raw scores from a verbal test for scaling purposes, and then preparing a conversion table incorporating age allowances, as is done for a standardized test;
(c)   using raw scores as in (b) but using the conversion table from the scaling verbal test instead of preparing a new one from the raw data.

Method (c) is the most convenient and easy to apply but is unlikely to be as accurate as the other two.

Table 11 shows the number of authorities who make age allowances when rank orders are obtained and which methods they use.

Table 11: *Authorities using different procedures for applying age allowances to teachers' assessments*

METHOD (described in text)	CCs No.	CBs No.	WALES No.	TOTAL No.	%
1. Method (a)	0	12	0	12	13
2. Method (b)	2	1	0	3	3
3. Method (c)	6	7	1	14	16
4. Other method	4	8	2	14	16
5. No age allowances applied	21	24	2	47	52
Total No. of LEAs concerned	33	52	5	90	100

One County Council gave no reply to the question analysed in Table 11.

There has been some increase since 1968 in the numbers and proportions of authorities using formal methods of applying age allowances. The number of authorities using method (a) has increased from seven to 12 and method (c) from 10 to 14. The number of authorities using no age allowance has decreased from 64 to 47. There are still, however, less than half applying age allowances to teachers' assessment.

5. *Record cards*

No major change in the use of record cards appears to have occurred. The absolute number of authorities using cards as information for selection purposes, apart from their use by teachers, has declined from 71 to 66, whereas of those authorities with a procedure, the proportion using cards has increased from 55 per cent to 63 per cent. The only interesting change is an increase from 15 to 21 of those authorities using cards for all candidates.

These results must, however, be treated with caution, for, although the question indicates use of record cards 'over and above reference to them in arriving at teachers' assessments', the practice in some authorities may not be easily categorized. Some authorities indicated difficulty in answering this question, especially where the procedure was largely in the hands of the teachers rather than a formalized procedure performed by the officials. It seems likely that record cards are an important part of many authorities' practices at various stages, though this is only surmised from the comments written in under this question.

Table 12: *Authorities using record cards in their allocation procedure*

	CCs	CBs	WALES	TOTAL	
	No.	*No.*	*No.*	*No.*	%
1. Used and consulted for all candidates	6	13	2	21	20
2. Used and consulted only for some candidates	15	20	1	36	34
3. Used and consulted only in exceptional cases	3	5	1	9	9
4. Not used at all	15	24	1	40	38
Total with procedure	39	62	5	106	100

Five authorities gave no reply to the question analysed in Table 12.

6. *Interviews*

Typically, record cards (Table 12) and interviews, with which this section deals, provide additional information on small numbers of pupils about whom some doubt remains after the basic allocation procedure has been applied. It is probably true that at this level of detail in allocation, the steps to be followed are not as strictly prescribed as elsewhere. As previously, a few authorities volunteered additional information which threw light upon the flexibility of approach to allocation. In particular, certain authorities queried the use of the phrase 'by interviewing teachers'. It was suggested that this implied that the procedure was formalized in a way that misrepresented the reality where teachers were more closely involved in the allocation. A possible indication of the changing role of the teachers is the evidence given in Diagram 5, that whereas the proportion of authorities interviewing pupils has steadily declined since 1960, the proportion of authorities interviewing teachers has increased. The downward trend in the interviewing of pupils is undoubtedly a result of the adverse evidence as to the value of interviewing for such purposes. The upward trend in the interviewing of teachers is perhaps an indication of the extent to which authorities are tending to consult them more as experts.

Diagram 5: *Trends in the percentages of authorities interviewing teachers and pupils*

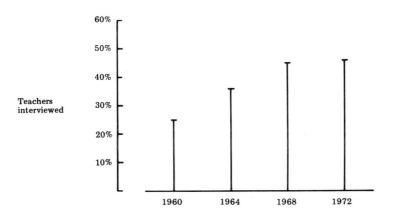

Teachers interviewed

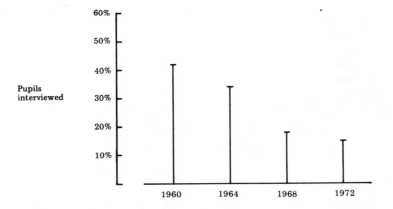

Pupils interviewed

Similarly, a distinction was suggested with reference to 'interviewing parents' between the practice of the authority and that of the schools. A meeting between parents and teachers may be normal in some authorities; particularly those authorities that follow a procedure known as 'guided parental choice'. In such cases, the formal structure of the questionnaire did not fit their practices. This again indicates a change in approach that may not be evident from the formal statistics.

The findings otherwise differ little from those of the previous study. The details are given in Tables 13, 14 and 15.

Table 13: *Authorities interviewing pupils as part of their allocation procedure*

	CCs	CBs	WALES	TOTAL	
	No.	No.	No.	No.	%
1. Some pupils interviewed	7	7	2	16	15
2. No pupils interviewed	34	56	3	93	85
Total with procedure	41	63	5	109	100

Table 14: *Authorities interviewing teachers as part of their allocation procedure*

	CCs	CBs	WALES	TOTAL	
	No.	No.	No.	No.	%
1. Some teachers interviewed	24	21	5	50	46
2. No teachers interviewed	16	42	1	59	54
Total with procedure	40	63	6	109	100

Table 15: *Authorities interviewing parents as part of their allocation procedure*

	CCs	CBs	WALES	TOTAL	
	No.	No.	No.	No.	%
1. Some parents interviewed	3	3	1	7	6
2. No parents interviewed	37	60	5	102	94
Total with procedure	40	63	6	109	100

The totals in Tables 13, 14 and 15 are 109, not 111, due to two authorities in each case not replying to the specific question. In Table 13 these are one English County Borough and one Welsh authority, in Tables 14 and 15 one English County Borough and one English County Council.

7. Sex differences

Evidence abounds that, at age 11, girls do better than boys in most attainment tests. It has therefore been recommended that the two sexes should be treated separately in any procedure. Despite this, a proportion of authorities have, in the past, considered sexes together, i.e. made reference to the same pass mark or standard when allocations were made.

Table 16 shows the position in 1972. The percentage of authorities treating sexes separately has remained fairly constant over the past 16 years and the position today is little different from 1968.

Table 16: *Authorities treating boys and girls separately and together*

	CCs	CBs	WALES	TOTAL	
	No.	No.	No.	No.	%
1. Together	13	11	3	27	25
2. Together in mixed schools, otherwise separately	6	1	2	9	8
3. Separately	21	51	1	73	67
Total with procedure	40	63	6	109	100

Two authorities gave no reply to the question analysed in Table 16.

8. Borderzone procedures

The proportion of authorities using borderzone procedures has altered little from the proportion in 1968. Indeed, there has been little variation since 1952. The proportion using a borderzone procedure has ranged between 73 per cent and 79 per cent during the 20 years. This report therefore will merely restate some of the points made in the previous study.

Some of the types of allocation evidence, such as essays and interviews in certain authorities, are only collected for a proportion of the candidates. Where this occurs, the individuals concerned are normally those in the borderzone group. These are defined for the purposes of the survey as consisting of a relatively small proportion of candidates about whom some doubt remains after the basic allocation procedure, and for whom additional evidence is considered necessary. The group would normally be thought of as of middling ability, spanning the cut-off point between those who are designated as suitable for grammar education and those who are not.

Less limiting definitions of 'borderzone' could be given. In the very broadest sense, all authorities must have a borderzone procedure, since there will always be a number of cases in need of review. Without going to this extreme, two types of procedure may not fall within the definition given and are therefore worth noting:

(a) Some authorities collect additional information, not for a middle doubtful group, but for the whole of the upper range. That is to say, on the basis of a small amount of information, such as a verbal test, a group of pupils, perhaps up to half of the age group, emerge as 'grammar possibles' and may go forward to take further tests.

(b) Some authorities use all the information they collect in making their initial selection decisions but, since their information may consist of test scores and/or teacher ratings, a number of corners have to be cut in arriving at a single criterion measure. The borderzone procedure of these authorities may then consist of re-examining the component parts of the criterion measure to discover, for example, large discrepancies between teacher ratings and test scores. This procedure does not, however, involve the collection of additional information.

In the questionnaire, authorities were asked to indicate whether they operated a borderzone procedure within the definition offered. A classification of replies is given in Table 16.

Table 17: *Authorities using borderzone procedure*

	CCs	CBs	WALES	TOTAL	
	No.	*No.*	*No.*	*No.*	*%*
1. Use borderzone procedure	34	45	5	84	77
2. No borderzone procedure	7	17	1	25	23
Total with procedure	41	62	6	109	100

Two authorities gave no reply to the question analysed in Table 17.

CHAPTER THREE

The Development of Comprehensive Systems

1. *Comprehensive systems*

When the last report was written, most authorities had a selective allocation procedure. It was, however, reported as being a time of change, with 104 authorities expecting to join the 26 that had already abolished allocation, though only 25 of them indicated that they had definite or even provisional plans to this end. As is now evident four years later, only 24 authorities have, in fact, abolished allocation.

What has happened, though, is that there has been a considerable increase in the number of authorities that have abolished procedures in at least part of their areas and an increase in the number that have some comprehensive schools. This distinction is made because 17 authorities with a procedure throughout their area have some comprehensive schools. As can be seen by reference to Table 1, 106 authorities have abolished allocation procedures in at least part of their areas for pupils entering secondary schools in September 1972, but as many as 117 authorities already had comprehensive schools for the year commencing September 1971. This section reports upon what systems have been introduced.

A major impetus to the growth of comprehensive schooling came from the directive 'The Organization of Secondary Education' (Department of Education and Science, Circular 10/65, 1965). This instructed Local Education Authorities to prepare and submit plans to reorganize secondary education along comprehensive lines. It gave details of six alternative schemes which are essentially the same as the categories given in this report. The extra groups in this report arise from sub-division of some categories. The Circular also made certain recommendations as to the suitability of various systems.

In particular, the schools of the type referred to as 'orthodox' comprehensive schools, 11 to 18, were recommended as providing 'the simplest and best solution'. This solution has clearly been widely accepted, with 91 authorities adopting this type of school as one of the systems in their area. This is similar to the position in 1968. Of those authorities with comprehensives, in that year 79 per cent had 11–18 comprehensives as one of their systems, they are now found in 76 per cent. This type of school is particularly common in Wales and in the English County

Councils. They have been adopted by 15 out of 16 of the former and 42 out of 43 of the latter authorities. The one type of system which has clearly increased in popularity is the middle school three-tier system, with transfer at ages 8/9 and again at 12/13. In 1968 this system was found in eight authorities; now 19 authorities have adopted it. Two DES Circulars have some bearing on this increase. Circular 10/65 indicated that 'the Secretary of State does not intend to give his statutory approval to more than a very small number of such proposals in the near future'. The following year Circular 13/66 stated 'The Secretary of State has therefore decided that while the questions whether there should be a national change in the age of transfer, and, if so, what the new age should be, must await the publication of the reports of the Central Advisory Councils for England and Wales and the Government's consideration of them, there are urgent practical reasons why a greater degree of flexibility should be allowed now to authorities. He will, therefore, regard a change in the age of transfer for the time being as a matter for local option, and he is prepared to consider proposals from authorities on this basis.' This system seems to be especially popular in the County Councils, being found in 15 authorities.

As one of the major problems of reorganization has been limitations imposed by the size of existing buildings, part of the appeal of the middle school system may be that it can be instituted without massive new buildings. In urban areas it will frequently have been possible to form new enlarged schools from two or more separate schools in close proximity. In the County Councils, schools in general are more widely dispersed, militating against the adoption of the all-through school.

The types of system given in Table 18 have been grouped under broader classifications. An important major distinction can be made between two major groups of systems which transfer pupils at some stage during their secondary education. Group I comprises those systems that are comprehensive throughout the years of compulsory schooling. When pupils transfer to a senior secondary school at 13 or 14 they move to another school with an all-ability intake. Group II comprises those systems where some pupils enter a selective school at this latter transfer age, so that pupils will in their last years be attending different types of school.

The middle school systems discussed above are normal examples of Group I with the third stage being fully comprehensive. The other systems in this group are those that still practise transfer at 11+ and then again at 13 or 14. There has been little change in the number of authorities with these systems. In 1968 there were 12 and nine authorities transferring at ages 13 and 14 respectively. The findings of the present survey are that the number of authorities with these systems are respectively nine and 14 in 1972. As with the middle schools, these have the advantage of reducing the size of schools and facilitating reorganization using existing buildings.

Those systems classified as Group II above can be categorized further into two groups. (1) Two authorities transfer all pupils at age 13 or 14 to new schools, using some selective criteria. Though the determining factor may be parental choice or the pupil's decision to continue his education

Table 18: *Authorities which have adopted different types of system*

	CCs	CBs	WALES	TOTAL
All-through				
1. 11/12 - 18	34	42	15	91
Group I *Where all pupils transfer* *at each stage*				
2. 11/13 - 13/18	2	3	4	9
3. 11/14 - 14/18	6	6	2	14
4. 8/9 - 12/13, 12/13 - 18	14	3	1	18
Group II *Where different pupils transfer* *to different schools or only* *some pupils transfer at ages* *between 11–16*				
5. 11 - 15/16 with some pupils transferring to senior high schools at 13/14	8	6	0	14
6. 8/9 - 12/13 and transfer to different types at 12/13	1	0	0	1
7. 11 - 13 and transfer to different types at 13	0	2	0	2
Other systems				
8. 11 - 16 and sixth-form colleges	6	6	0	12
9. Any other system	6	2	3	11
Total number with comprehensive schools	58	43	16	117

beyond the school leaving age, this system involves some form of selective allocation. (2) In the other system, pupils transfer to a secondary school at 11 and then, at a second transfer age 13 or 14, some pupils remain in the same school, whereas others are allocated to a senior high school. This practice is essentially similar to the pre-1944 system, whereby some pupils were selected for grammar schools from elementary schools. This now occurs in 14 authorities compared with eight in 1968.

The other main system is that with comprehensive schooling up to the school leaving age, followed by sixth-form colleges. The number of authorities with this system has increased from eight to 12. Finally, there are 11 authorities that have systems which do not fit the categories given. In some instances these involve a practice where some schools are 11 – 15/16 and others 11–18, with pupils transferring to the 11–18 schools for sixth-form work.

What is clear is that a considerable diversity of practice exists. The next section considers certain other aspects of this. In particular, the extent to which authorities have a mixture of systems. Table 18 gives the analysis of the different types of system being adopted.

2. *A multiplicity of systems*

As is evident from Table 18 indicating the different types of comprehensive schools adopted by authorities, not only is there considerable diversity as to the system in operation, but some authorities also have a mixture of systems within their area. This section investigates this diversity in more detail.

The diversity of systems is indicated by the following factors:

(1)   Whether allocation procedures are used.
(2)   What proportion of pupils in the appropriate age group experience an allocation procedure.
(3)   What type of comprehensive systems exist, and hence at what different ages many pupils change schools.
(4)   How many types of comprehensive systems co-exist in one authority.
(5)   Where comprehensive and other schools co-exist:
         (i)   what is the relationship between the catchment areas of each type of school;
         (ii) which pupils are assessed by the authorities.

The numbers of authorities using allocation procedures was considered in the section on eligibility. As was indicated there, the authorities divided into approximately equal numbers of those with a procedure throughout, with a procedure in part of their area, and with no procedure. It is those authorities, mostly County Councils, with a procedure in only part of their area, which can be expected to exhibit most diversity.

The proportions of pupils in the authorities who experience a procedure was also determined and the results of this are given in Table 19.

Table 19: *Authorities using an allocation procedure for different proportions of their pupils*

	CCs	CBs	WALES	TOTAL
None	6	33	11	50
Under 20%	0	2	0	2
20% – 40%	3	4	1	8
40% – 60%	12	3	1	16
60% – 80%	13	0	1	14
80% – 100%	5	7	0	12
All	5	46	1	52
No reply	3	2	2	7
Total	47	97	17	161

Seven authorities gave no reply to this question

From Table 19 it is clear that most of these authorities with a procedure in part of their area practice a selective allocation procedure for over half their pupils. An estimate was therefore made as to what proportion of the total age group undergo selection. A small number of authorities either did not reply to this question or did not return the questionnaire. Figures were therefore available for 690,000 pupils compared with a total age group of 710,000 pupils in maintained schools.

The total number of pupils recorded by the authorities as undergoing a procedure was 440,000. This, on the assumption that the non-response is not atypical, gives an estimate of 64 per cent of the total age group.

From the Table 18 section, it is clear that the age of transfer for different systems varies considerably and pupils may experience a change of school at almost any age after eight. The distribution of types of systems was given in Table 18. From the figures it is evident that some authorities have a number of systems. The extent of this was therefore determined. This is given in Table 20. In most authorities only one type of system has been adopted.

Table 20: *Total number of comprehensive systems co-existing in one authority*

NUMBER	CCs No.	CBs No.	WALES No.	TOTAL No.	%
1	22	47	9	78	67
2	11	10	6	27	23
3	7	1	0	8	7
4	3	0	1	4	3
Total	43	58	16	117	100

There are, however, 39 authorities with two or more systems and, as might be expected, 21 of these are County Councils, indicating their greater internal diversity. In three cases there are as many as four different systems; 49 per cent of County Councils with comprehensives have more than one system, compared with only 19 per cent of County Boroughs.

Where authorities do have both comprehensive and selective schools, it is interesting to inquire how these are distributed into catchment areas and to what extent there is transfer between areas with different systems.

Authorities were asked which of three alternative arrangements existed in their area:

(1) A system, where, within the same catchment area, comprehensive and maintained selective schools co-exist.

(2) A system where comprehensives and selective schools existed in separate catchment areas and no transfer occurred between areas. This is a system where comprehensives exist without competition for pupils with selective schools.

(3) A system where comprehensives and selective schools exist in separate catchment areas and transfer between areas occurs as a normal practice.

In the above classification, direct grant schools are not included, as allocation to them is in general distinct from the local authority procedure. These schools may therefore co-exist with any of these arrangements. The findings are given in Table 21.

Table 21: *Authorities with a mixture of selective and comprehensive schools*

TYPE OF SYSTEM	CCs	CBs	WALES	TOTAL	
	No.	No.	No.	No.	%
1. Comprehensive and selective in same catchment area	2	16	0	18	25
2. Separate catchment areas, no transfer	27	6	4	37	52
3. Separate catchment areas, transfer	3	4	1	8	11
4. Other	6	2	0	8	11
Total with mixed systems	38	28	5	71	100

The difference between the County Councils and the County Boroughs is interesting. Within the County Councils, 27 out of 38 authorities had distinct catchment areas, with no transfer between areas. Only two said they had comprehensive and selective schools co-existing in the same area. The six authorities indicated under 'other' in general had an arrangement more complex than the classification would allow, with more than one of the features given above. Within the County Boroughs, however, 16 out of 28 indicated that they had comprehensive and selective schools co-existing in one catchment area. These differences can possibly be attributed to the greater size and the larger number of sub-divisions in the County Councils compared with the County Boroughs. The finding for the County Boroughs is possibly an indication of the extent to which old established grammar schools are found in these authorities and have been retained.

3. *Which pupils are assessed*

The preceding section showed that comprehensive and selective schools co-exist in many authorities, in some within the same catchment area, in others in distinct catchment areas. It was therefore of interest to consider which pupils are assessed by these authorities. A question asked authorities with both types of school to indicate whether they tested:

(1)   all pupils;
(2)   only pupils in selective areas;

(3)　pupils in the selective areas and others outside the area whom their parents or teachers wish to be considered for selection;

(4)　only pupils whose parents or teachers wish to be considered for selection;

(5)　any other practice.

The results are given in Table 22.

Table 22: *Which pupils are assessed in authorities with a mixture of systems*

	CCs	CBs	WALES	TOTAL	
	No.	No.	No.	No.	%
1. All	3	16	1	20	28
2. Only pupils in selective area	17	5	5	27	38
3. Pupils in selective area and others wishing to be selected	13	3	0	16	22
4. Only those wishing to be selected	1	3	0	4	6
5. Other practice	2	2	0	4	6
Total with mixed systems	36	29	6	71	100

As is evident, the County Boroughs tend to have a common practice throughout their area. Sixteen assess all pupils and a further three assess only those wishing to be selected. By contrast, among English County Councils only three authorities test all pupils, whereas 17 assess pupils in selective areas and others wishing to be considered for selection.

The small number of Welsh authorities, themselves mostly County Councils, are similar to the English County Councils.

A further analysis was made, relating which pupils were assessed to the arrangement of selective and comprehensive schools. The alternative arrangements were the same as those given in Table 21. This analysis is given in Table 23.

Table 23: *Authorities with mixture of systems and type of pupil following procedure*

	Relationship between Comprehensive and Selective Schools				
	1 Same area	2 Different areas, no transfer	3 Different areas, transfer	Others	Total
All	12	2	2	1	17
Only pupils in selective area	0	23	1	2	26
Pupils in selective area and those wishing selection	1	10	3	1	15
Only those wishing to be selected	3	0	0	1	4
Other	1	0	1	2	4
Total	18	37	8	8	66

10 authorities answered only one of the two questions tabulated.

As might be expected, there is a relationship between testing all pupils and the co-existence of comprehensive and selective schools in the same catchment area. Twelve authorities fall into this category and 11 of these are County Boroughs. Also of interest are authorities with comprehensives and selective schools in different areas who do not practise transfer between areas except in special circumstances. If no transfer is practised, one would expect only those pupils in the selective area to be assessed. Twenty-three authorities fall into this category. It is not clear, however, why 10 authorities, while not practising transfer, do test other pupils whose parents or teachers wish them to be considered for selection. There may be some problem here of ambiguity of interpretation of the question.

CHAPTER FOUR

Forecasts and Implications

The previous survey asked some questions about future plans. This time it was felt there was a need for slightly more detail. The tentative nature of some of the results should, however, be stressed. There is a series of stages through which plans must pass before they can take effect and there is no longer a situation where authorities have a directive to produce them.

Questions were asked to enable us to assess both the immediate and the long-term situation relating to schools reorganization. There were three questions concerning changes in the short term. The first asked authorities whether they had reorganization plans to take effect in September 1972. This was followed by questions:

(1)   to determine whether this created a complete comprehensive system or altered the proportion of pupils entering comprehensive schools and

(2)   to determine the types of schools being introduced. The classification of types of school was the same as for existing comprehensive systems.

Analysis of these are given in Tables 24, 25 and 26.

Table 24: *Authorities that are not already comprehensive and have reorganization plans*

	CCs	CBs	WALES	TOTAL	
	No.	No.	No.	No.	%
Yes	27	25	6	58	54
No	14	36	0	50	46
Total	41	61	6	108	100

Three County Boroughs did not answer the question analysed in Table 24.

Table 25: *What the effect of reorganization plans will be*

SYSTEM	CCs No.	CBs No.	WALES No.	TOTAL No.
Complete comprehensive system	2	9	2	13
Increase in comprehensives	25	11	4	40
Increase in selective schools	0	1	0	1
Change in types of comprehensive school	0	3	0	3
Total with plans	27	24	6	57

One County Borough did not answer questions analysed in Tables 25 and 26.

Fifty-eight authorities indicated that they have reorganization plans, though in 40 of them this will only result in an increase in comprehensive schools. Only 13 will have achieved a complete comprehensive system by 1976. In line with the present situation, the County Councils continue their trend towards a comprehensive system, but only one out of 27 will complete the process by then. In contrast, nine County Boroughs will go completely comprehensive.

One large County Council described its situation as:

'(1) Agreement to dispense ultimately with 11+.
(2) Rejection of any uniform reorganization.'

This situation seems to be not uncommon among similar authorities. Reorganization in small compact homogeneous County Boroughs can be fairly rapidly achieved, but for larger authorities, particularly those with a number of divisions, the process is undoubtedly complex and lengthy.

A number of authorities also made special mention of Roman Catholic schools. In some authorities these schools were already comprehensive. Elsewhere they were not included in general schemes for reorganization. The number of these schools and their relation to the maintained school system may affect the ease with which total comprehensive systems are introduced.

Again, from Table 26 it can be seen that the types of system being adopted are distributed much as at present. The 11–18 comprehensive is the predominant pattern with the standard middle school pattern and the sixth-form college as the main alternative. The figures suggest that there may be

Table 26: *Comprehensive systems being adopted*

TYPE OF SYSTEM	CCs No.	CBs No.	WALES No.	TOTAL No.
All-through 1. 11/12 – 18	15	12	4	31
Group I *Where all pupils* *transfer at each stage*				
2. 11/12 13/18	0	2	0	2
3. 11/14 14/18	1	1	0	2
4. 8/9 – 12/13, 12/13 – 17	7	2	2	11
Group II *Where either pupils transfer* *to different schools or only* *some pupils transfer at ages* *between 11 – 16*				
5. 11 – 15/16 with some pupils transferring to senior high schools at 13/14	0	1	0	1
6. 8/9 – 12/13 and transfer to different types at 12/13	1	0	0	1
7. 11/13 and transfer to different types at 13	0	1	0	1
Other systems				
8. 11/16 and sixth-form colleges	5	3	3	11
9. Any other system	4	3	0	7
Total number of authorities adopting comprehensive systems	27	23	6	56

One County Borough did not answer questions analysed in Tables 25 and 26.

some trend towards adopting sixth-form colleges.

Two questions on long term plans asked whether there were any future reorganizations and when reorganization would be completed.

Seventy-nine authorities indicated they had plans for future reorganization towards a complete comprehensive system beyond 1972–73. Of these,

35 were County Councils, 40 County Boroughs and four Welsh authorities. Only 13, however, indicated a specific year when they expected this to be complete and, of these 13, 12 are County Boroughs and one a County Council. Table 17 indicates spread of the reorganization over time.

Table 27: *The year authorities expect to complete reorganization*

YEAR	1973/74	1974/75	1975/76	1976/77
NO. OF AUTHORITIES	3	4	3	3*

*the one County Council included here.

It seems evident that the rate of complete reorganization has slowed down and the main aspect of the trend is towards increasing numbers of comprehensives in authorities with mixed systems rather than total reorganization. The situation will however be totally altered by the Local Government Reorganization.

On the basis of replies to the survey, it seems likely that there will be only a slight increase in the number of authorities with no allocation procedure by 1976. Of the 13 authorities going totally comprehensive in September 1972, 12 have already abolished selective allocation during the survey year 1971-72 and are included in the 50 with no procedure. The one other authority going comprehensive in 1972 plus the 13 giving definite dates for the completion of reorganization suggest that by 1976-77 the total number without any allocation procedure will have increased from the present figure of 50 to 64.

One other point of interest concerning reorganization and the future structure of comprehensive schools was brought out in a comment by one authority. Asked whether there was anything concerned with allocation not covered by the questionnaire, this reply was given.

'The question of allocation of pupils to individual comprehensive schools, especially when reorganized schools have different origins, traditions and public images. Zoning has been attempted to ensure, for an initial period in this authority, that all schools have an equal chance to achieve a new ethos and a new image, given parity of mixture in terms of social backgrounds, etc.'

This question should perhaps be considered more fully in a future survey.

Conclusion

The previous survey saw the preceding four years as a 'time of change'. There was also some evidence to suggest that substantial changes were to be expected in the succeeding years.

As is now evident, the process of total reorganization has in fact occurred in only a few authorities. The process of changeover towards comprehensive education appears to be slowing down.

The picture for the next few years seems to be one of very gradual reorganization toward comprehensive education, with many authorities continuing to maintain mixed systems of selective and comprehensive schools.

Summary

1. The trends from 1968 to 1972 are for the most part a continuation of trends in the preceding period.

2. 111 out of 163 authorities are still using allocation procedures. The proportion of authorities using some procedures remained stable, whereas the use of certain other methods has declined markedly.

3. Among these authorities, verbal reasoning tests and teacher assessments remain the almost universal means of allocation.

4. Practices in relation to borderzones, sex differences and the use of interviews and record cards show no major changes.

5. The use of mathematics and English attainment tests and of essays continues to decline.

6. The major changes expected by the last report have not occurred. Only 24 authorities have abolished allocation procedures since 1968.

7. There has been a marked increase in the number of authorities, particularly County Councils, with a mixture of comprehensive and selective systems.

8. The all-through 11–18 school remains the most popular pattern for comprehensives in existence and in future plans, though both the middle school and the sixth form college show some increase in popularity.

9. There is evidence of a slowing down of change to comprehensive education.